MEGALODON AND OTHER
PREHISTORIC SHARKS

BY TAMMY GAGNE

raintree
a Capstone company — publishers for children

Raintree is an imprint of Capstone Global Library Limited, a company incorporated in England and Wales having its registered office at 264 Banbury Road, Oxford, OX2 7DY – Registered company number: 6695582

www.raintree.co.uk
myorders@raintree.co.uk

Edited by Carrie Sheely
Designed by Dina Her
Original illustrations © Capstone Global Library Limited 2022
Picture research by Kelly Garvin
Production by Tori Abraham
Originated by Capstone Global Library Ltd
Printed in China

978 1 3982 2279 3 (hardback)
978 1 3982 2278 6 (paperback)

British Library Cataloguing in Publication Data
A full catalogue record for this book is available from the British Library.

Acknowledgements
We would like to thank the following for permission to reproduce photographs: Alamy/Marty Snyderman/Stephen Frink Collection, 20; BluePlanetArchive.com/Makoto Hirose/e-Photo, 27; Capstone Press/Jon Hughes, 9; Newscom: De Agostini Picture Library Universal Images Group, 5, Stephen J. Krasemann/NHPA/Photoshot, 6; Science Source: Christian Darkin, cover, Corey Ford/Stocktrek Images, 21, Gwen Shockey, 18, Jaime Chirinos, 11, 12, 14, 23, 24, JAMES KUETHER, 26, Jeffrey Rotman, 8; Shutterstock: Cq photo juy, 1, frantisekhojdsz, 29, wildestanimal, 28; Wikimedia/Danielle Dufault/PLOS Journals, 17

Every effort has been made to contact copyright holders of material reproduced in this book. Any omissions will be rectified in subsequent printings if notice is given to the publisher.

All the internet addresses (URLs) given in this book were valid at the time of going to press. However, due to the dynamic nature of the internet, some addresses may have changed, or sites may have changed or ceased to exist since publication. While the author and publisher regret any inconvenience this may cause readers, no responsibility for any such changes can be accepted by either the author or the publisher.

CONTENTS

Words in **bold** are in the glossary.

CHAPTER 1

An amazing discovery

Imagine finding remains of one of the most powerful creatures that ever lived! In 1867, a man called Jay Terrell did just that. He and his son were visiting the shores of Lake Erie in the United States. While there, Terrell discovered a **fossil** of what he called a "terrible fish". The fossil was from a type of **prehistoric** shark. It was one of the fiercest prehistoric sharks. Scientists named the shark *Dunkleosteus terrelli* partly after Terrell.

Long ago, the middle of North America was covered by water. *Dunkleosteus terrelli* swam through this shallow sea. This shark lived about 360 million years ago. It grew up to 6 metres (20 feet) long and weighed more than 1 tonne. It was about the same size as a modern great white shark.

Dunkleosteus terrelli was a fierce hunter
of the seas in prehistoric times.

FACT

Scientists think there have been only two animals with stronger
jaws than *Dunkleosteus terrelli*. These are the alligator and the
Tyrannosaurus rex dinosaur.

A model of *Dunkleosteus terrelli* skull

People who visit the Cleveland Museum of Natural History in the United States can see the fossil of a *Dunkleosteus terrelli* skull. It includes two sets of fang-like teeth and sturdy jaws. This shark used its sharp teeth and strong jaws to hunt other fish.

Dunkleosteus terrelli died out millions of years ago. But modern sharks are related to this shark and other prehistoric sharks. Modern sharks **evolved** over time. They share many features with their prehistoric relatives, such as fins and sharp teeth. But some sharks that lived millions of years ago had very different features. A few looked very odd!

FACT

Sharks are among the oldest animals on the planet. They lived long before dinosaurs, insects or even trees!

CHAPTER 2

The biggest prehistoric sharks

Films about sharks often focus on the biggest and fiercest modern **species,** such as great whites. If films had existed in prehistoric times, other giant sharks would have been the stars!

The tooth of a great white shark (left) and the tooth of a megalodon (right)

Megalodon's strong jaws and sharp teeth helped make it a skilled hunter.

Megalodon

Megalodons were the largest sharks that ever lived. Most megalodons measured about 15 m (50 feet) long. But scientists think that some reached 25 m (82 feet) long! The biggest megalodons could have weighed up to 70 tonnes. That's the weight of about 10 male African elephants. The biggest modern hunting sharks are great whites. They can reach 6.4 m (21 feet) long.

Megalodons died out about 2.6 million years ago. Scientists are not sure why. Some think it was because of climate change. This could have caused the **prey** of megalodons to die out. Megalodons needed a lot of food to survive. They ate the largest seals and turtles in the ocean. Scientists think that eventually the animals did not have enough to eat.

Scientists also think climate change could have made the water temperatures cooler. They think megalodons had to maintain a high body temperature. They would have had to stay in warmer waters to hunt and raise their young. Some prey, such as whales, could have moved to the cooler waters easily. But megalodons wouldn't have been able to move to cooler waters.

A megalodon attacks a whale.

Modern whale migration and megalodons

Megalodons may be the reason whales **migrate** today. Modern whales such as humpback whales move to cooler waters seasonally. Whales could have begun doing this to get away from megalodons. Whales were probably the main prey of megalodons. People have found whale fossils with megalodon teeth stuck in them.

Scientists believe the Ginsu shark's tail helped it reach fast speeds to catch prey.

FACT

The Ginsu shark was named after a popular knife because of its teeth. The Ginsu knife is known for being especially sharp.

Ginsu shark

Ginsu sharks lived about 100 million years ago. They were the largest sharks of their time. They measured up to 7 m (23 feet) long. These sharks had hundreds of razor-sharp teeth. Their teeth helped the sharks become fierce **predators**. Ginsu sharks made mcals of fish that were bigger than they were. These sharks also ate the largest sea turtles that ever lived, *Archelon ischyros*. The turtles grew to about 3.7 m (12 feet) long.

Ptychodus

Sharks in a group called *Ptychodus* lived more than 85 million years ago. These sharks grew to about 10 m (33 feet) long. They had many flat teeth. Scientists think these sharks may have had up to 1,000 teeth in their jaws! Their flat teeth would have helped them crush shellfish. Experts think these sharks mainly lived near the seafloor.

A scissor-tooth shark swims near a large school of fish.

Scissor-tooth shark

Scissor-tooth sharks lived about 300 million years ago. They measured about 6.1 m (20 feet) long. This is about the size of modern great whites. But the mouths of scissor-tooth sharks looked completely different from those of great whites. These sharks had two curved arcs of teeth. Each one pointed outwards.

Scissor-tooth sharks also hunted differently from other sharks. Most sharks kill prey by biting. But scientists think scissor-tooth sharks thrashed their heads up and down instead. This movement created slashing wounds on the other animals. Sometimes it would slice prey in half.

CHAPTER 3

Small prehistoric sharks

Many modern sharks are small. One type is smaller than your hand! Many prehistoric sharks were small too. These smaller sharks had some things in common with their larger relatives. But they often differed from them in more ways than just size.

Spiny shark

Spiny sharks lived about 360 million years ago. These fish had skeletons made of cartilage. Modern sharks also have skeletons made from this material. Cartilage is softer than bone. Spiny sharks were named after the spiny pieces of cartilage that helped support their fins.

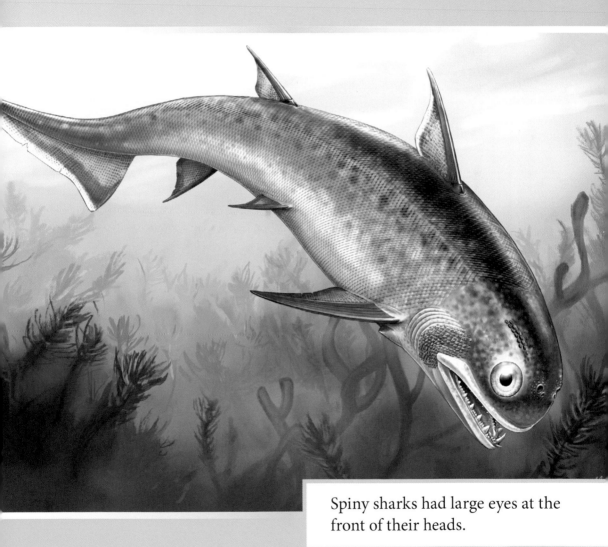

Spiny sharks had large eyes at the front of their heads.

Spiny sharks in the *Climatius* group had two fins on the top of their backs and several fins underneath their bodies.

Spiny sharks rarely grew to more than 30 centimetres (12 inches) in length. They didn't look or behave like miniature versions of today's sharks. They had small heads and long bodies. They looked far less fierce. Spiny sharks had large eyes and short snouts. They used sight far more than their sense of smell.

Spiny sharks were filter feeders. This meant they trapped tiny food particles from the water with their gills. Pieces of cartilage in the gills helped make this process work. Although spiny sharks were small, they were the largest filter feeders alive at the time.

Pristiophorus striatus

Being small didn't stop some prehistoric sharks from being great hunters. *Pristiophorus striatus* lived between 5 and 23 million years ago. It was about 1.1 m (3.5 feet) long. It had an extra-long snout lined with sharp teeth to tear prey. Other types of sharks with these features still exist today. Scientists call them saw sharks.

Modern saw sharks such as longnose saw sharks have long snouts like their prehistoric relatives did.

A group of *Xenacanthus* sharks

Xenacanthus

Sharks in the group *Xenacanthus* lived about 360 million years ago. Sometimes they are called eel sharks because they looked like eels found in modern oceans. The sharks had small heads and long, narrow bodies like today's eels. They measured about 1 m (3.2 feet) long.

Unlike other sharks, *Xenacanthus* had a long, ribbon-like fin that ran the length of its body. It also had a sharp spine on the back of its skull. The shark probably used this body part for protection.

FACT

Like other sharks, *Xenacanthus*'s skeleton was made of cartilage. But the spine on its skull was made of bone. Scientists think the spine was **venomous**. The venom would have harmed predators.

CHAPTER 4

Sharks with unusual features

Each prehistoric shark was unique. But some had especially unusual features. If you had seen these sharks, you probably would have done a double take!

Scaleless shark

The scaleless shark swam through Earth's waters 380 million years ago. It didn't have a fierce appearance. It had a small head and a thin body. It measured about 1.2 m (4 feet) long. It was also much less muscular than many other sharks at the time.

The scaleless shark was named after its most obvious feature. Unlike most other sharks, it had no **scales**. Its thin skin made it harder for the scaleless shark to defend itself. But having no scales also made the animal much lighter and faster. It used its speed to catch prey.

Scaleless sharks had long, streamlined bodies to help them swim quickly.

Some scientists think the front dorsal fins on male anvil sharks might have been used to attract females.

Anvil shark

The anvil shark was among the oddest-looking sharks. It lived more than 300 million years ago.

The male anvil shark had a dorsal fin on its back that was flat on top. The anvil shark was named after the iron block that this dorsal fin looked like. The fin was covered in **denticles**. Modern sharks still have these small, tooth-like scales all over their skin. The top of the anvil shark's head also had denticles.

Bandringa

Sharks in the group *Bandringa* lived about 310 million years ago. Their standout feature was a long, spoonbill-shaped snout. Adults grew to about 3 m (10 feet) long. Their snouts stretched up to half their body length. The sharks might have used these snouts to dig out buried prey at the sea floor.

Buzzsaw shark

The buzzsaw shark wasn't actually a shark.
But it was a relative of modern sharks. Also called
Helicoprion, this fish lived about 290 million years
ago. It was named after its unusual tooth pattern. The
fish's teeth were arranged in a spiral pattern. This
made its mouth look like the blade of a circular saw.
The appearance was so odd that it took scientists a
long time to work out what its fossils actually were.
At first, many thought they were looking at ancient
seashells.

Helicoprion did not have upper
teeth. It relied on its spiral teeth
for attacks.

A modern goblin shark swims in the deep sea.

Goblin shark

Fossils of the goblin shark are much easier to identify. This shark had a long, flat snout that extended forward. It also had a highly unusual jaw. It could come unhinged when the animal ate large prey. Goblin sharks still exist today. They have been around for 125 million years!

A great white shark swims through the ocean near Guadalupe Island, Mexico.

Understanding sharks

Studying prehistoric sharks helps people understand modern sharks better. The sharks that swim through today's oceans get many of their traits from their ancient relatives. Large jaws, big dorsal fins and sharp teeth are common traits of both modern and prehistoric sharks.

Over time, many sharks evolved to better match their environments. Prehistoric hammerhead sharks first lived about 20 million years ago. Today, several hammerhead species still exist. They look a lot like their prehistoric relatives. But scientists think they have better eyesight and sense of smell than the hammerheads of long ago. They use these senses for finding food.

Each shark has evolved in its own interesting way. We can't go back to see the sharks that swam the seas millions of years ago. But if you could, which one would you want to see?

A great hammerhead shark hunts for food.

Glossary

cartilage strong, bendable material that forms some body parts of people and animals

denticle small, tooth-like scale that covers a shark's skin

evolve change gradually over time

fossil remains or traces of plants and animals that are preserved as rock

migrate travel from one area to another; some animals move from one area to another to find warmer weather

predator animal that hunts other animals for food

prehistoric from a time before history was recorded

prey animal hunted by another animal for food

scale one of the small, hard plates that covers the skin of most fish and reptiles

species group of animals with similar features

venomous able to produce a poison called venom

Find out more

Books

Fish (Animal Classification), Angela Royston (Raintree, 2015)

Sharks and Other Deadly Ocean Creatures: Visual Encyclopedia, DK (DK Children, 2016)

Shark vs Killer Whale (Animal Rivals), Isabel Thomas (Raintree, 2018)

The Ultimate Book of Sharks, Brian Skerry (National Geographic Kids, 2018)

Websites

www.bbc.co.uk/cbbc/shows/shark-bites
Learn about many different types of sharks.

www.dkfindout.com/uk/animals-and-nature/fish/sharks
Find out more about sharks and take the Fish: true or false quiz!

www.dkfindout.com/uk/dinosaurs-and-prehistoric-life/prehistoric-fish
Find out more about prehistoric fish.

Index